Nikolai MEDTNER

PIANO CONCERTO No. 1
Op. 33
(1917)

SERENISSIMA MUSIC, INC.

INSTRUMENTATION

2 Flutes
2 Oboes
2 Clarinets (B-flat, A)
2 Bassoons

4 Horns (F)
3 Trumpets (B-flat)
3 Trombones
Tuba

Timpani
Piano solo

Violin I
Violin II
Viola
Violoncello
Bass

Duration: ca. 35 minutes

First Performace: May 12, 1918
Moscow: Special Symphony Concert
Nikolai Medtner, piano solo
Segei Koussevitzky, conductor

ISBN: 1-932419-77-2

Printed in the USA
First Printing: August, 2007

PIANO CONCERTO No. 1

Op. 33

Nikolai Medtner
(1917)

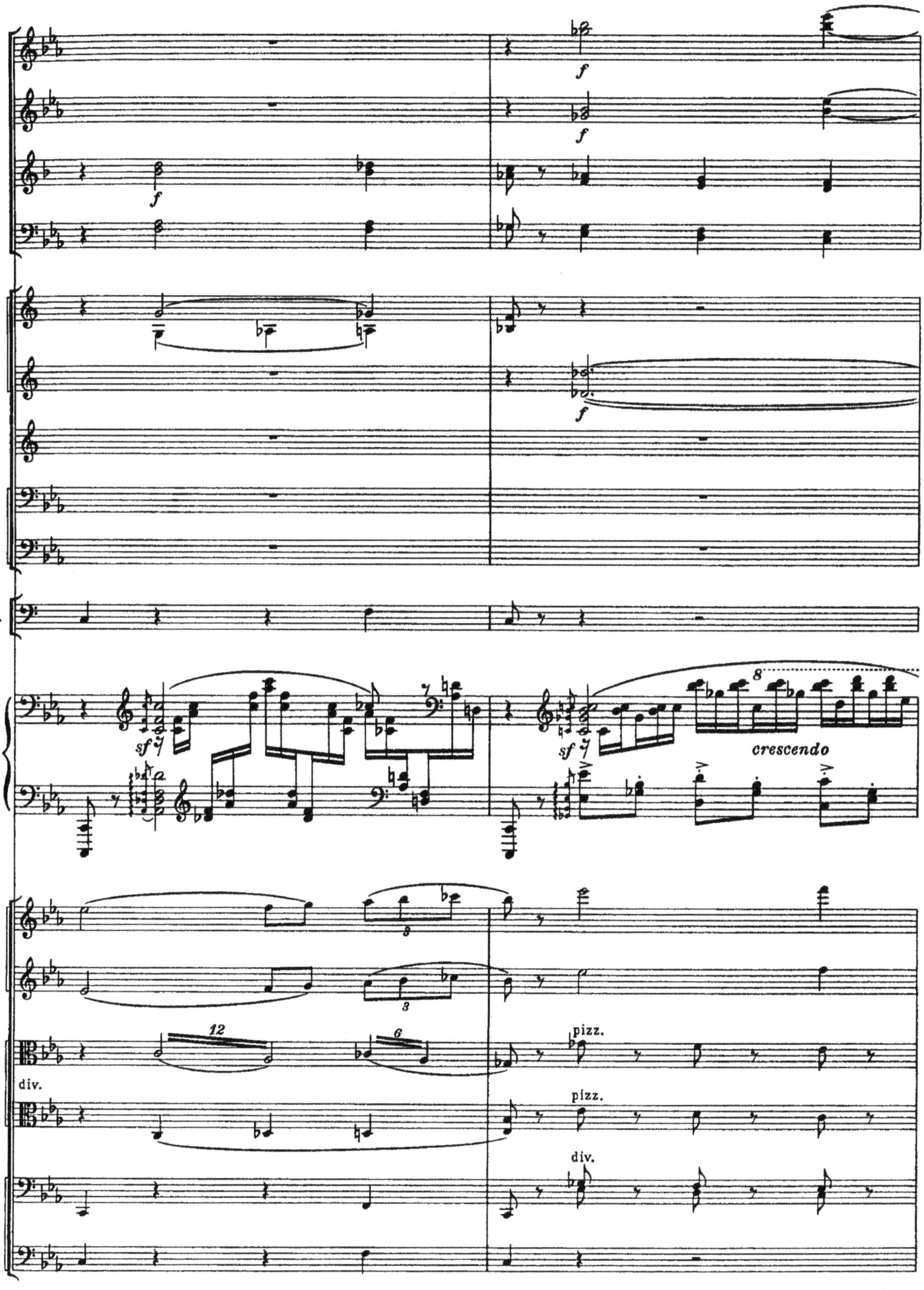
Fl.
Ob.
Cl.
Fag.
Cor.
Tr-be
Tr-ni e Tuba
Timp.
P-no
Archi
f
sf
crescendo
8
3
12
6
div.
pizz.

9

10

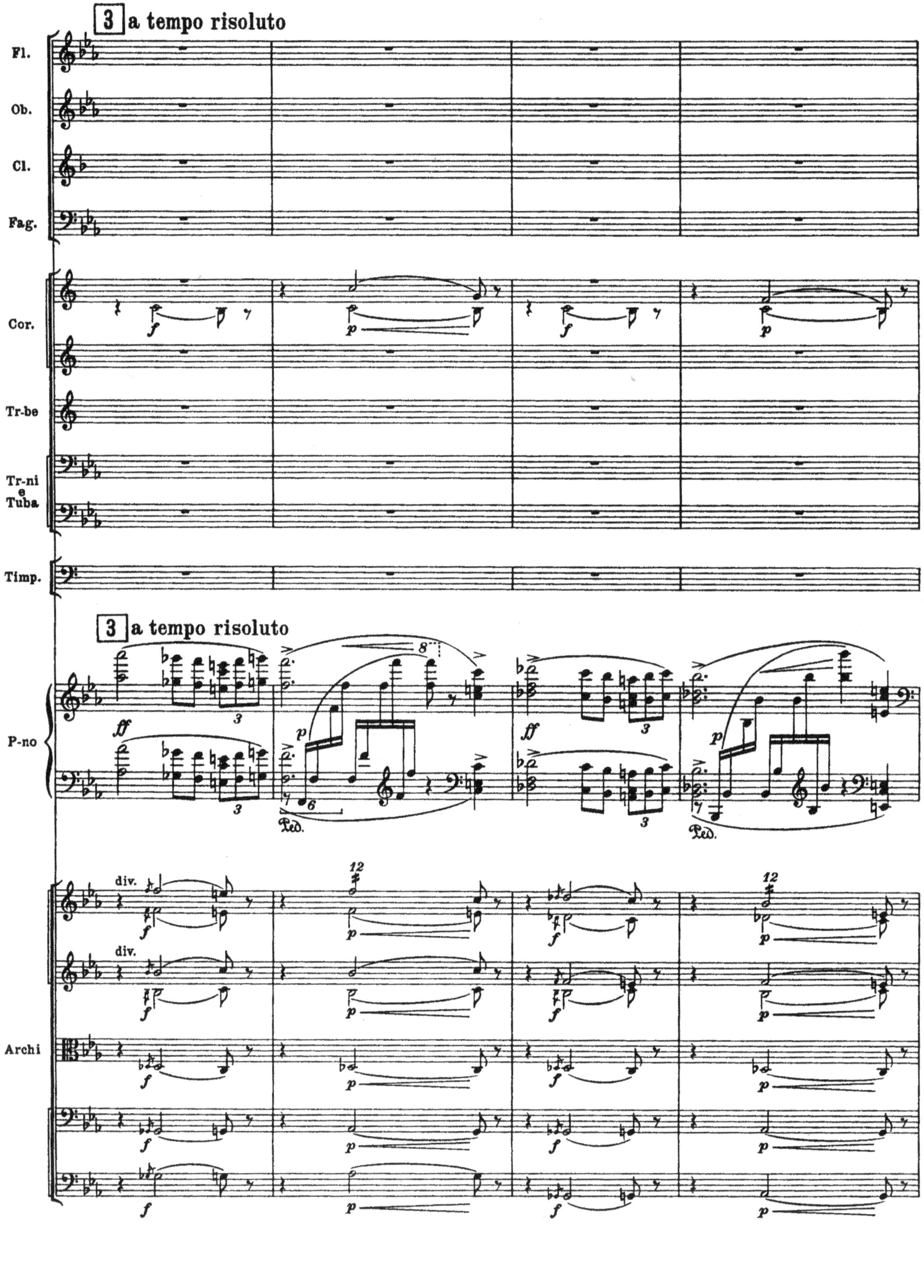
3 a tempo risoluto
Fl.
Ob.
Cl.
Fag.
Cor.
Tr-be
Tr-ni e Tuba
Timp.
3 a tempo risoluto
P-no
Archi
div.
div.
ff
p
f

17

18

20

e poi poco a poco a tempo

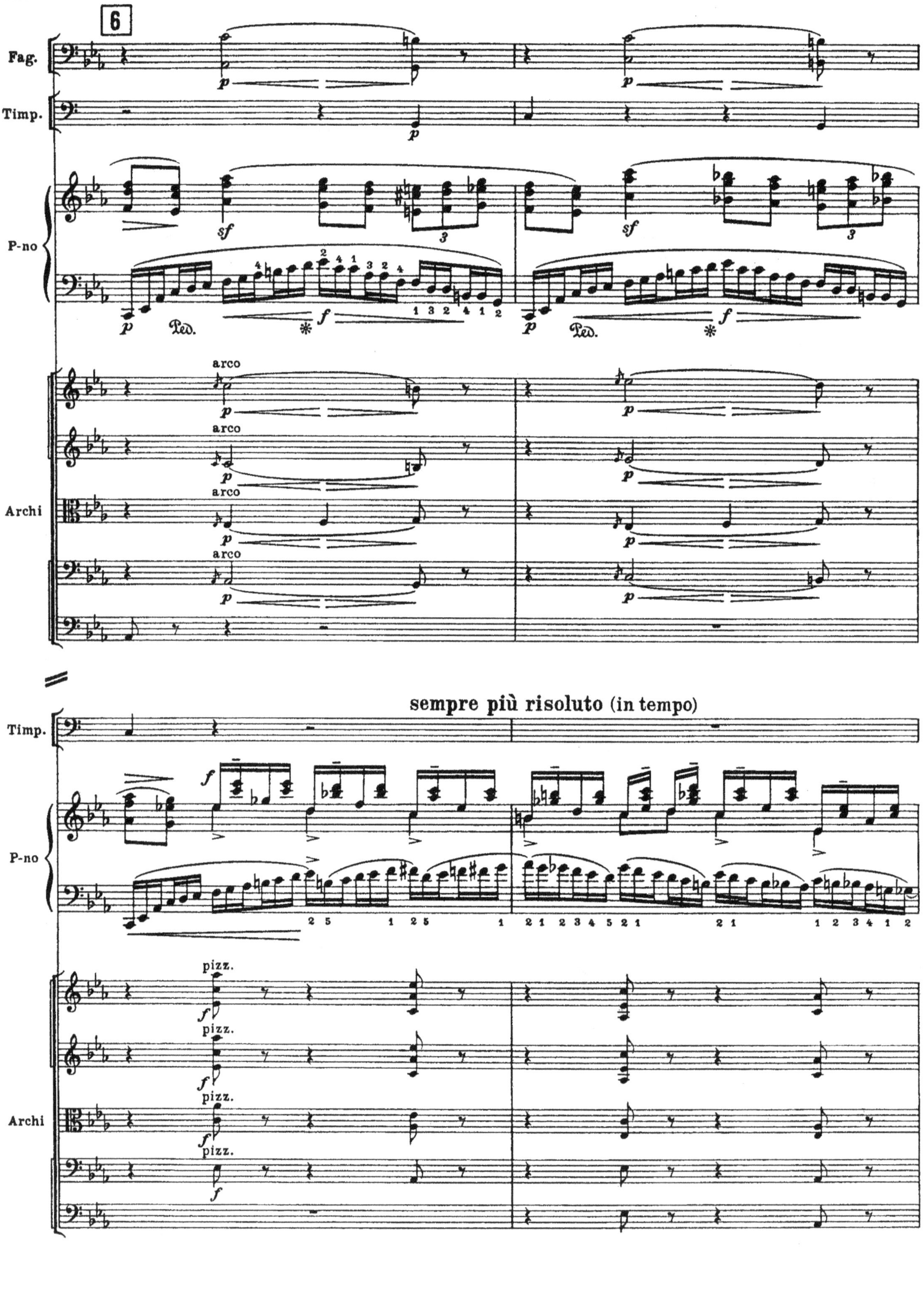
6
Fag.
Timp.
P-no
Ped.
arco
Archi
sempre più risoluto (in tempo)
pizz.

24

32

36

41

44

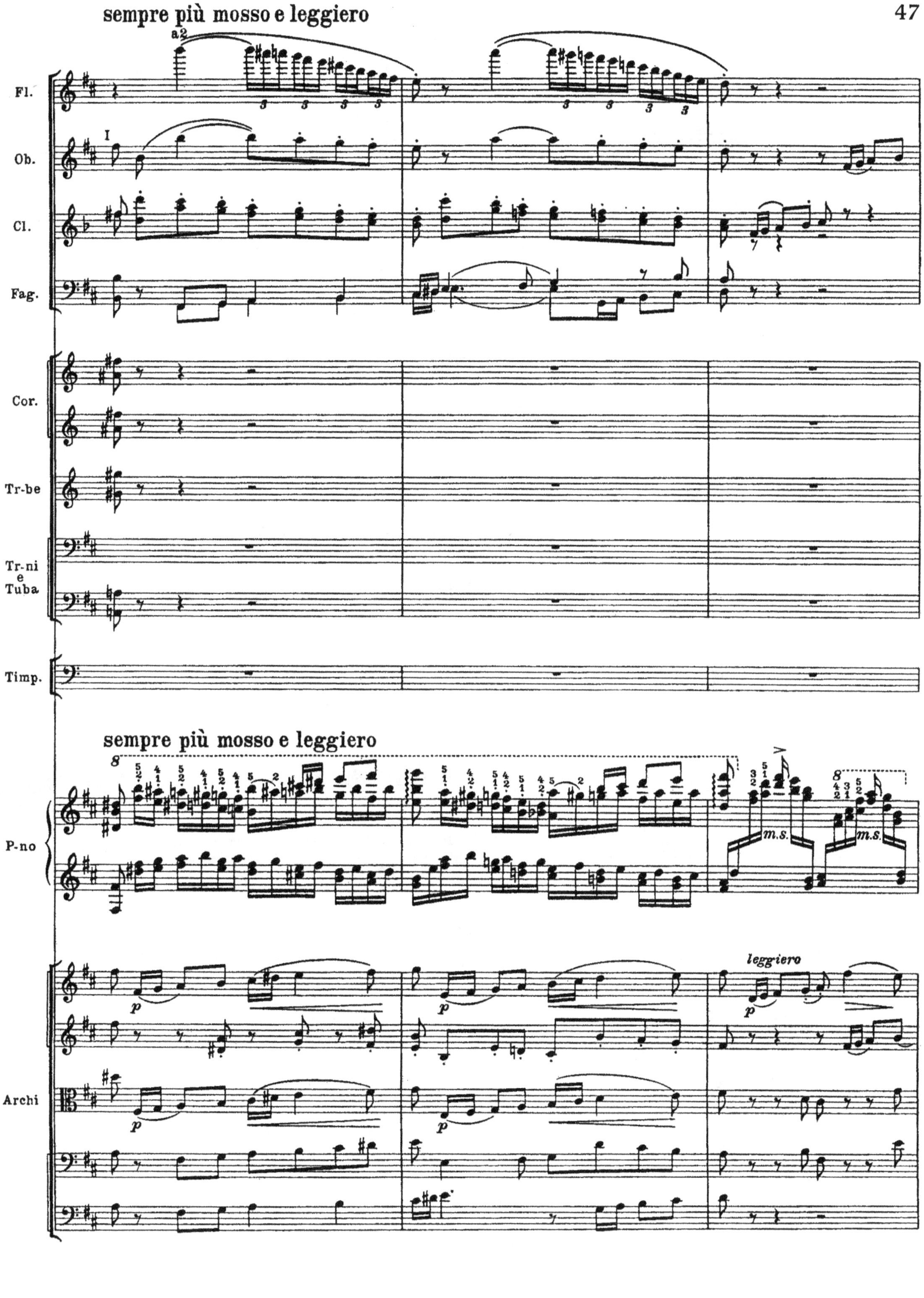
sempre più mosso e leggiero
a2
I
Fl.
Ob.
Cl.
Fag.
Cor.
Tr-be
Tr-ni e Tuba
Timp.
sempre più mosso e leggiero
m.s.
m.s.
P-no
leggiero
p
p
p
p
Archi

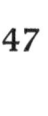

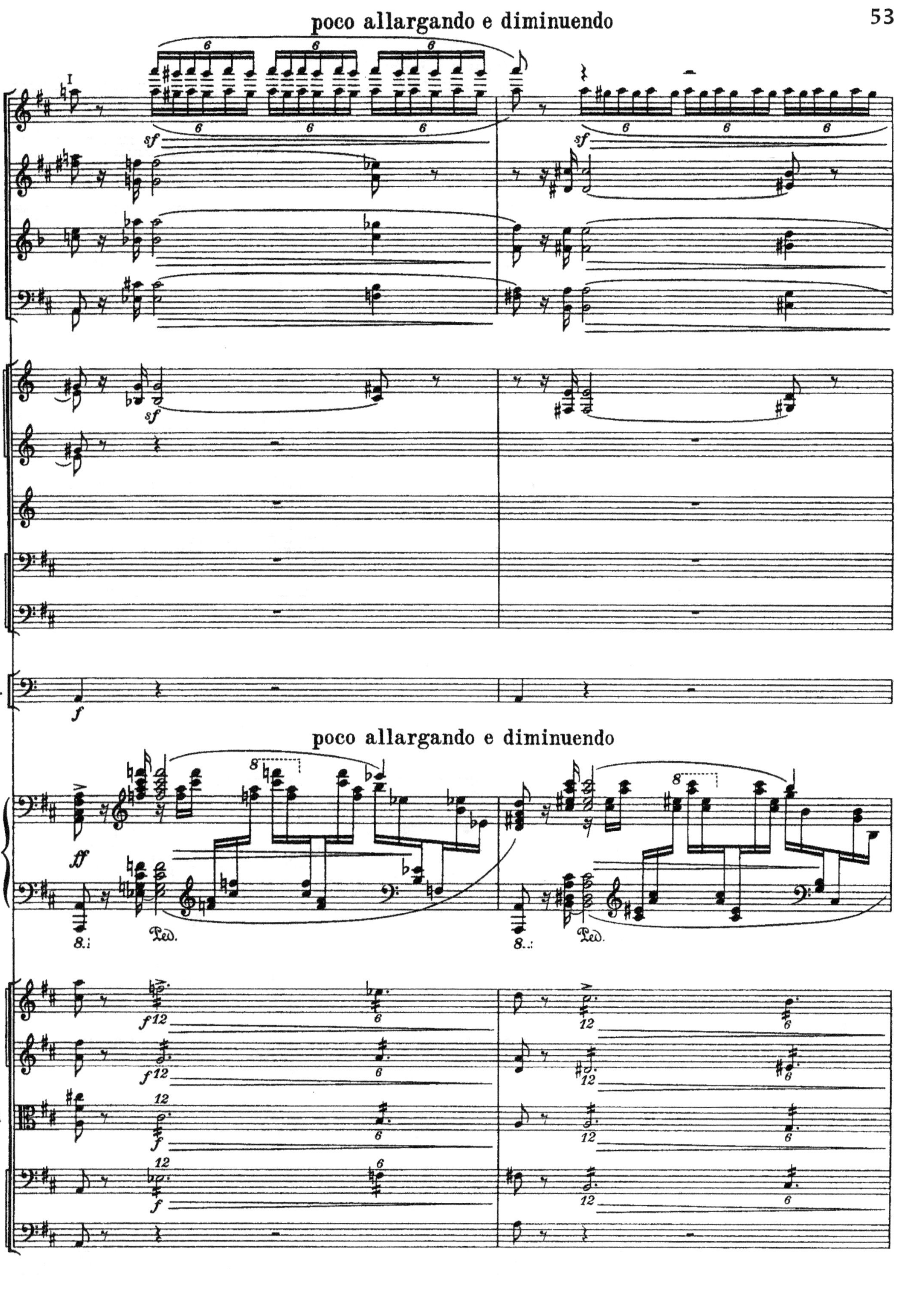
poco allargando e diminuendo
Fl.
Ob.
Cl.
Fag.
Cor.
Tr-be
Tr-ni e Tuba
Timp.
poco allargando e diminuendo
P-no
Archi

58

62

*) The trill should start before the half-beat.

64

68

72

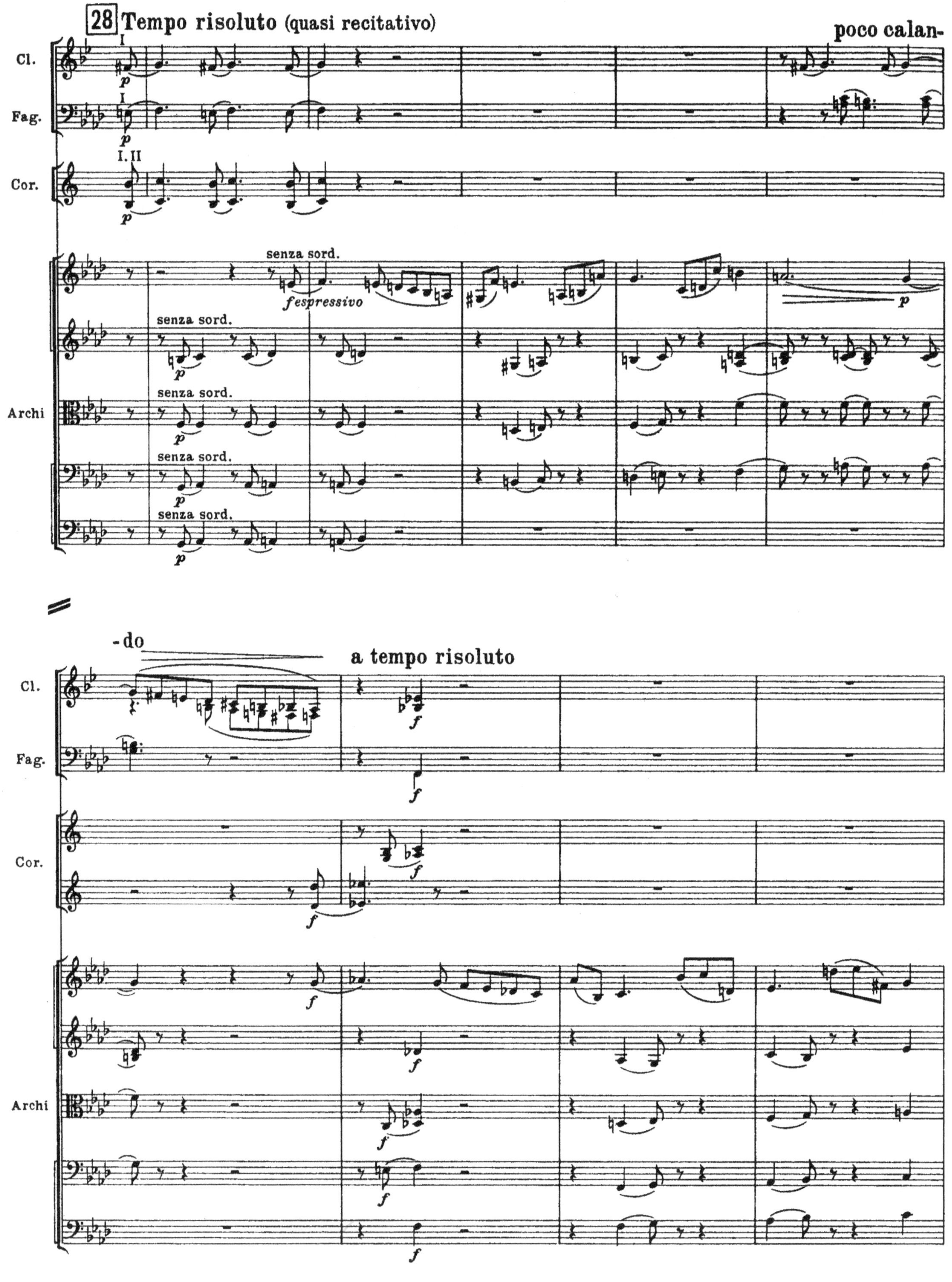
28
Tempo risoluto (quasi recitativo)
poco calan-
Cl.
Fag.
Cor.
Archi
I
I
I. II
p
senza sord.
fespressivo
-do
a tempo risoluto
f

75

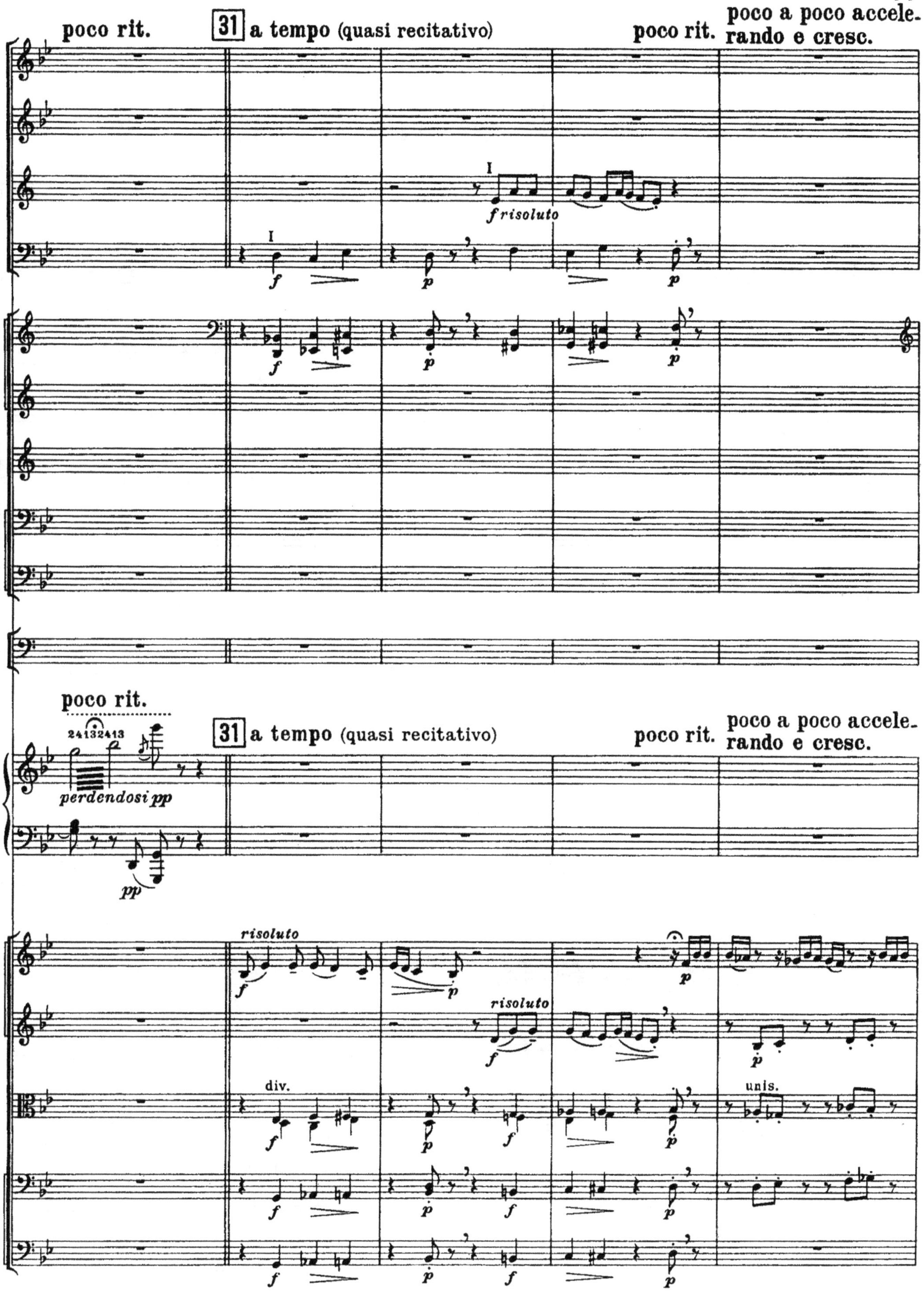
poco rit.
31 a tempo (quasi recitativo)
poco rit.
poco a poco accelerando e cresc.
Fl.
Ob.
Cl.
I
f risoluto
Fag.
I
f
p
p
Cor.
f
p
p
Tr-be
Tr-ni e Tuba
Timp.
poco rit.
24132413
31 a tempo (quasi recitativo)
poco rit.
poco a poco accelerando e cresc.
P-no
perdendosi pp
pp
Archi
risoluto
f
p
p
risoluto
f
p
div.
unis.
f
p
f
p
f
p
f
p
f
p
f
p

78

90

92

94

102

104

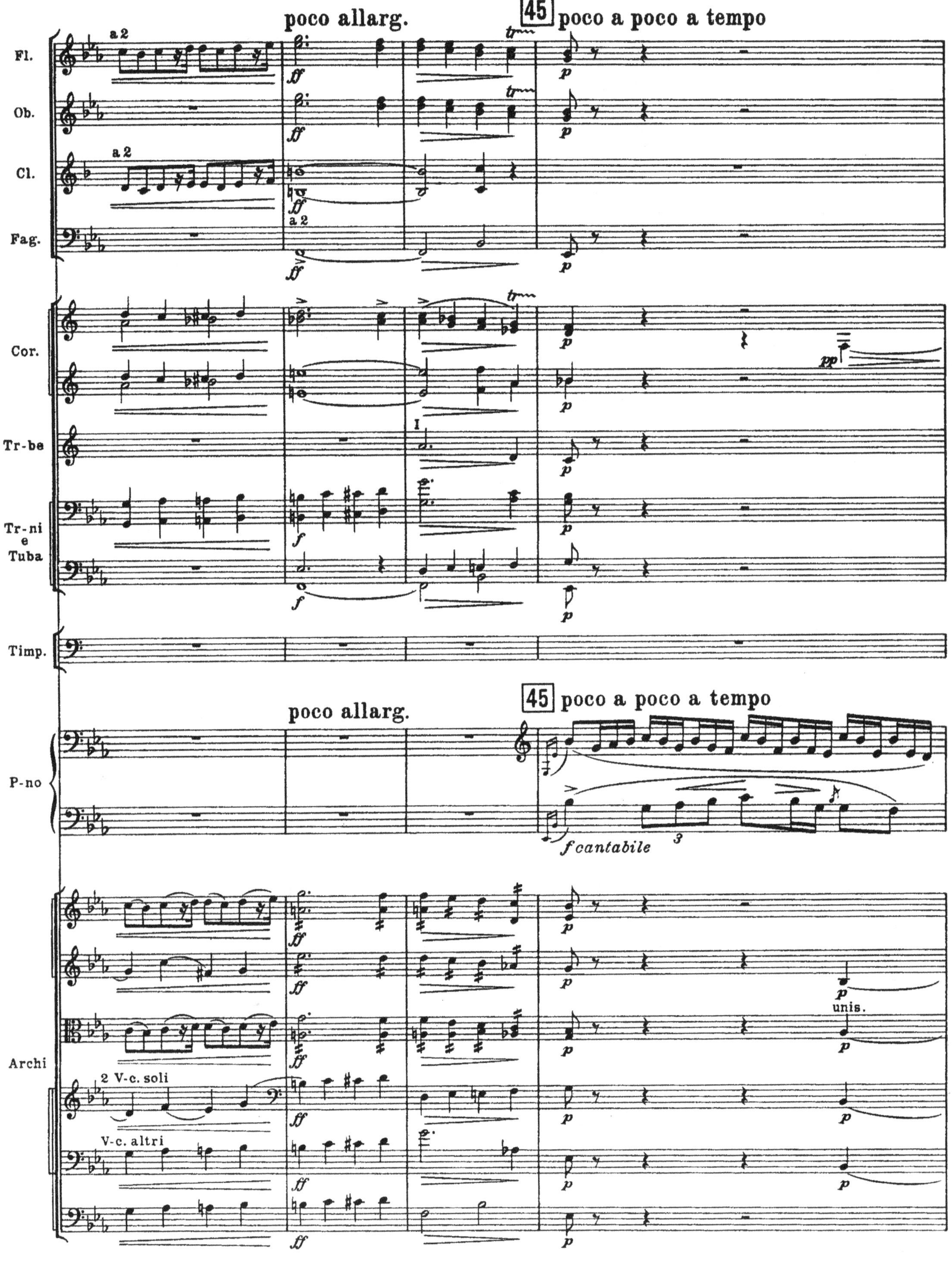
poco allarg.
45
poco a poco a tempo
Fl.
Ob.
Cl.
Fag.
a 2
ff
p
Cor.
pp
Tr-be
I
Tr-ni e Tuba
f
Timp.
P-no
f cantabile
3
Archi
2 V-c. soli
V-c. altri
unis.

110

112

114

49 affanato, ma al rigore di tempo

118

120

130

134

Coda

141

142

144

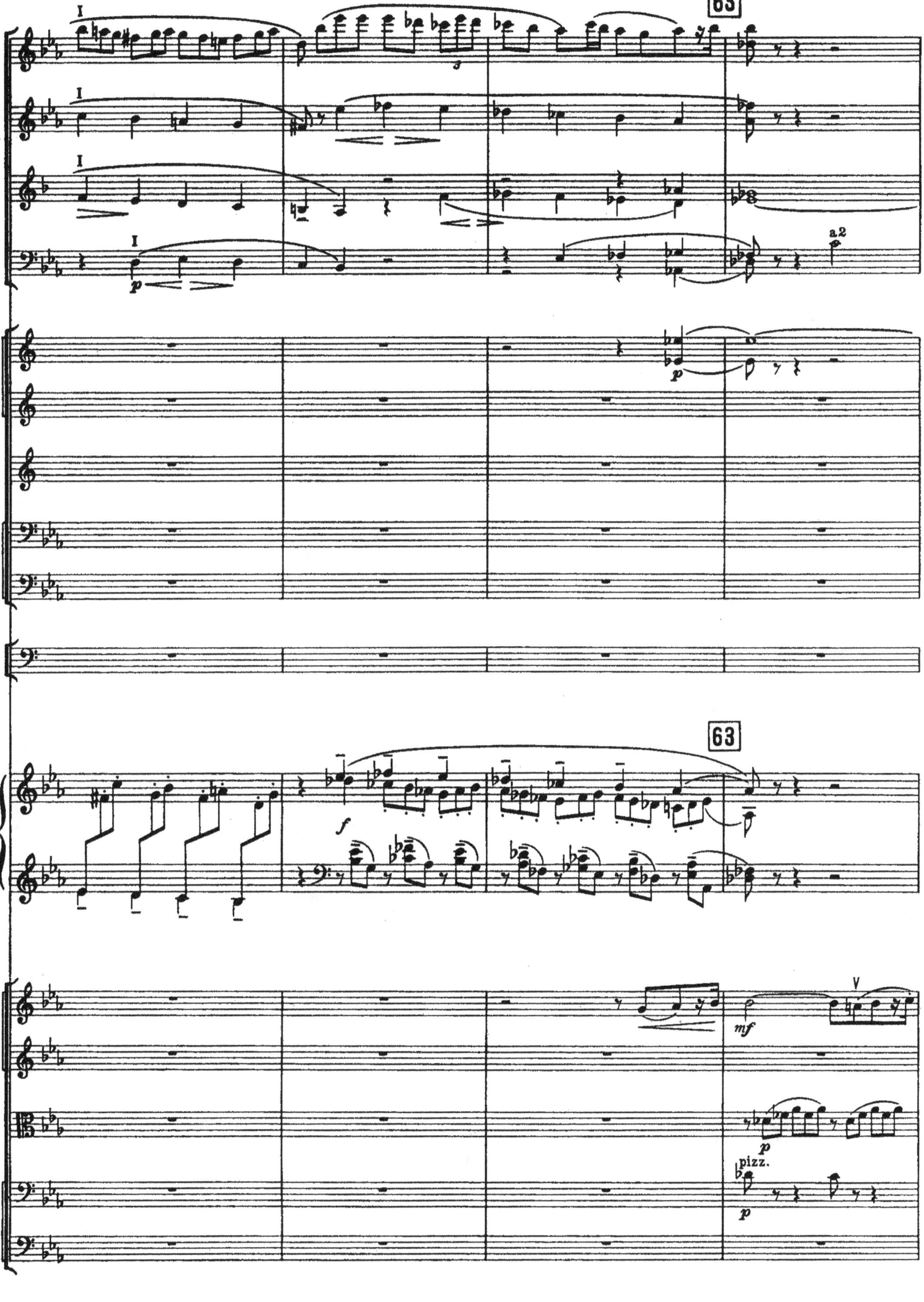
Fl.
Ob.
Cl.
Fag.
Cor.
Tr-be
Tr-ni e Tuba
Timp.
P-no
Archi
63
a 2
pizz.

148

155

156

157

158

160

162

163

164

diminuendo
Fl.
Ob.
Cl.
Fag.
Cor.
a2
Tr-be
Tr-ni e Tuba
Timp.
diminuendo
P-no
Ped.
Ped.
ossia
Archi

167

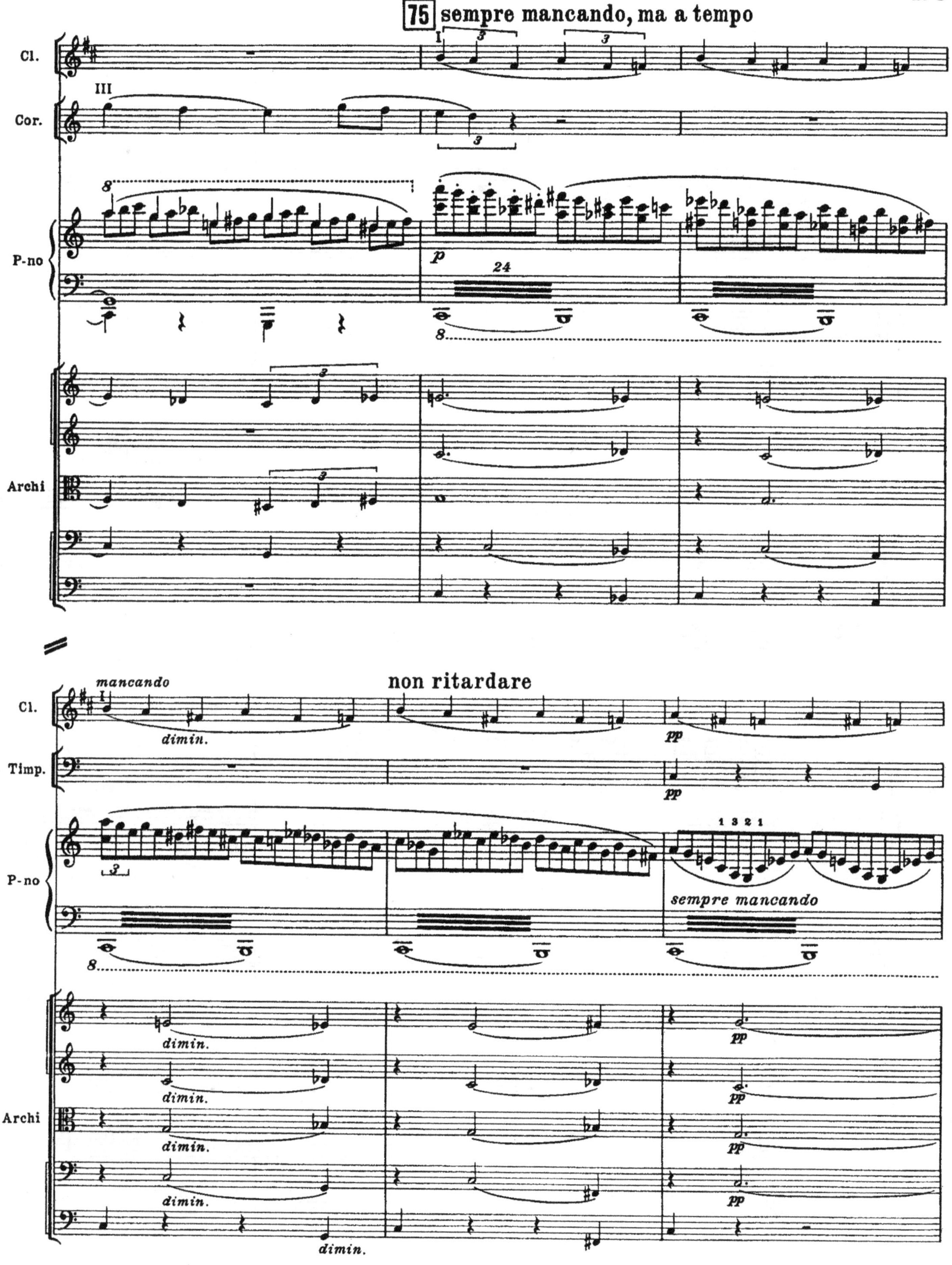
75
sempre mancando, ma a tempo
Cl.
Cor.
P-no
Archi
p
dimin.
mancando
non ritardare
pp
Timp.
sempre mancando
dimin.

176

www.ingramcontent.com/pod-product-compliance
Lightning Source LLC
Chambersburg PA
CBHW081838170426
43199CB00017B/2770